ROYAL
BALLET

Ballet
Spectacular

*A young ballet lover's guide
and an insight into a magical world*

— LISA MILES —

BARRON'S

BARRON'S

First edition for the United States and Canada published in 2015 by Barron's Educational Series, Inc.

Copyright © 2014 Carlton Books Limited

First published in 2014 by Carlton Books Limited
An imprint of Carlton Publishing Group
20 Mortimer Street, London,W1T 3JW, United Kingdom

All inquiries should be addressed to:
Barron's Educational Series, Inc.
250 Wireless Boulevard
Hauppauge, New York 11788
www.barronseduc.com

ISBN: 978-0-7641-6745-4
Library of Congress Control No.: 2014940905

Executive Editor: Anna Brett
Design Manager: Emily Clarke
Designer: Ceri Hurst
Production: Marion Storz

Manufactured by RRD, South China, Dongguan, China
Date of Manufacture: August 2014

9 8 7 6 5 4 3 2 1

Printed in China

The publishers would like to thank the following sources for their kind permission to reproduce the pictures in this book.
Key. t = top, b = bottom, l = left, r = right & c = center

CONTENTS

THE AMAZING
ART of BALLET

BALLET IS A HIGHLY SKILLED FORM OF DANCE THAT IS BOTH beautiful to watch and wonderful to take part in. The dancers are artists—who use their bodies, rather than words or music, to tell stories to the audience or simply to show what amazing things the human body can do when performing.

Ballet today

The art of ballet has developed over several hundred years, from a formal kind of dancing that only happened at royal courts, to today's ballets, which are designed for anybody to come and watch. It is a style of dance that is loved everywhere, with many top international ballet companies and famous dancers bringing ballet to a worldwide audience.

Learning ballet

Many top dancers begin learning ballet when they are very young—sometimes only five years old. However, you don't need to become a top dancer to enjoy learning ballet. Ballet dancing is a fantastic hobby that keeps your body fit and strong, teaches you how to express yourself to all kinds of music and, above all, lets you have lots of fun!

Going to the ballet

Watching a live ballet performance is an incredible experience. The whole event can be spectacular—from the dancers' skills, to the live music, amazing sets, and stunning costumes. If you are thinking of going to watch ballet, there are several kinds to choose from. If you can, it is often worth going to watch a triple bill. This is a performance in which you will get to see three one-act ballets. This way, you can watch a variety of dance in one program.

※ STORY BALLETS
These are ballets, often shown in three acts, that tell a story. Many famous **story ballets** originate from the 19th century, such as *The Sleeping Beauty*, choreographed by Marius Petipa.

Kristen McNally as Carabosse in the 2011 performance of **The Sleeping Beauty**, *a story ballet.*

※ THEME BALLETS
These are ballets that don't tell a story but convey a theme. For instance, *Jewels* is a **theme ballet** in three acts by George Balanchine, linked by the theme of gemstones—emeralds, rubies, and diamonds.

Samantha Raine in "Emeralds" from George Balanchine's Jewels, a theme ballet.

Yasmine Naghdi and James Hay in Christopher Wheeldon's **Polyphonia**, *an abstract ballet.*

※ ABSTRACT BALLETS
Abstract ballets have no story or strong theme. Instead they are designed to show off the dancers' techniques and how they can make their bodies form strong shapes and exciting movements. *Polyphonia* is an abstract ballet by Christopher Wheeldon.

- CINDERELLA -

In Frederick Ashton's ballet *Cinderella*, there is a wonderful moment in Act II where Cinderella enters the ball. She descends a set of steps **on pointe** and then takes tiny, rapid steps to the front of the stage, wearing a beautiful flowing cloak. This image shows Marianela Nuñez as Cinderella and Thiago Soares as The Prince in *Cinderella* for The Royal Ballet in 2010.

CHAPTER ONE

HISTORY OF BALLET

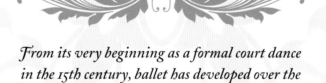

*From its very beginning as a formal court dance
in the 15th century, ballet has developed over the
years to the art form that we see today.*

*Opposite: Marie Taglioni (1804–84), center,
one of the first famous ballerinas.*

HOW
BALLET
BEGAN

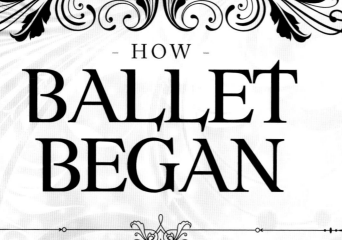

BALLET HAS ITS ORIGINS IN THE 15TH AND 16TH CENTURIES, at the royal courts of Italy and France. The courts were splendid places where high standards of dress and behavior were expected from the courtiers (the nobles who served the royal family). Courtiers were taught how to dance elegantly, as music and dancing were important parts of court entertainments.

*One of Louis XIV's most famous dancing roles was Apollo, Greek god of the sun, in the **Ballet de la Nuit**. He took the image of the sun as his emblem and for this reason he is known as the Sun King.*

The Sun King

In 1643, Louis XIV came to the French throne. He was an avid dancer and it was during his reign that ballet developed as an art form. He set up the Académie Royale de Danse, which taught specific steps to professional dancers for his court. Then, in 1669, Louis opened an opera house in Paris and ballets were performed as part of operas by professional dancers. At first, only men were allowed to dance in theaters but in 1681, women were allowed to dance professionally too.

The first ballets

Spectacular court entertainments had elaborate scenery and stage effects. The courtiers danced in heels and highly decorated costumes. The audience often watched from galleries, so the dancers were taught certain steps and patterns that could be appreciated from above. These dances were the first ballets, known as **ballets de cour** or court ballets.

Le Ballet Comique de la Reine, considered to be the first ballet, performed at the French court in 1581. It was based on the myth of the Greek goddess Circe.

Marie Camargo

Ballets began to be performed separately from operas, but dancers were still wearing heavy costumes and shoes with heels, as they did in the ballets de cour. Then, in the mid-18th century, Marie Camargo caused a big stir. She was the first ballerina to shorten her skirts so that the audience could see her calves and ankles, and she wore flat ballet slippers to improve her technique.

Marie Camargo, celebrated ballerina of the 18th century.

Romantic ballets

In the early to mid-19th century, an artistic movement called Romanticism had a strong influence on writing, painting, and music. It aimed to make people feel strong emotions, based on excitement and the beauty of wild nature.

Romanticism had an effect on ballet, too, and **Romantic ballets** of this period often have two settings—a "real" world and a "ghostly" one. Not many ballets survive from this period, but ones that are still popular are *La Sylphide* and *Giselle*. The second acts of these Romantic ballets are known as "white acts." In these acts, the dancers are all dressed in white to represent the ghostly world.

Tutus and pointe shoes

One important change in Romantic ballets was that the ballerina became a focal point for the ballet. Before this, male dancers danced the more important parts. Female dancers began to wear a costume now referred to as the Romantic tutu—a long, layered skirt that showed the feet and lower legs.

The most famous dancer of this period is Marie Taglioni. She was the first ever to dance on pointe—balancing on the very tips of the shoes. Dancing on pointe lengthens the line of the legs and feet, giving the impression that the dancer is floating.

Marie Taglioni in a Romantic tutu and pointe shoes.

CLASSICAL BALLET

During the late 19th century, ballet continued to develop in Britain, France, Italy, and Russia. At this time, ballet techniques became formalized, with specific body, arm, and leg positions, which became known as the Classical style.

Pyotr Il'yich Tchaikovsky (1840–93), composer of some of the greatest music ever created for ballet.

The Russian Classical ballets

Ballet became immensely popular in Russia particularly, meaning that some of the best **Classical ballets** came from this country, including *The Nutcracker*, *Swan Lake*, and *The Sleeping Beauty*. These three ballets in particular are still included in the **repertories** of top ballet companies today and huge audiences flock to see them. One of the reasons why they have survived for so long is that the music was created by the great composer Pyotr Il'yich Tchaikovsky, who wrote the amazing scores and directly influenced the creation of the ballets.

Creating the ballets

To accompany Tchaikovsky's music, Marius Petipa and Lev Ivanov created complex dance steps that were built into the story to show off the dancers' techniques. People who create dance steps are called **choreographers**. The dances were excuses to show off the dancers' skills, with the story told in **mime** gestures. A large group of dancers, known as the **corps de ballet**, provided the decorative background for the ballets.

Classical technique

In Classical technique, ballerinas dance on pointe, while both male and female dancers turn their legs out from the hips and point their toes, which extends their legs to make them look very long. They also have flexible upper bodies and raise their legs very high, with exciting turns, leaps, and difficult holds. Dancers perform complex solos and **pas de deux** (set pieces for two dancers).

Her feet are pointed, extending her legs and making them look long and elegant.

Hands and arms are held out elegantly. Here, the hand is poised above the head.

Eyes are looking at the audience.

Both dancers have their legs turned out from the hips.

Alina Cojocaru and Rupert Pennefather in "Diamonds" from George Balanchine's Jewels.

The ballerina is on pointe.

*The Prince (Steven McRae) holds Princess Aurora (Sarah Lamb) in the fish dive position from a pas de deux in **The Sleeping Beauty**. This is a difficult hold to achieve and requires perfect timing and confidence in your partner.*

His body is erect with arm raised.

Classical tutu

Due to the fact that dancers' leg- and footwork was becoming so complex, the Classical tutu began to be worn. It was a lot shorter and stiffer than the Romantic tutu and showed off the dancers' whole legs, as well as being easier to dance in. Ballerinas were now overshadowing their male counterparts, whose role it was to present the ballerina to the audience.

*Sarah Lamb in a Classical tutu from **Swan Lake**.*

- LA BAYADÈRE -

La Bayadère is a Classical ballet, choreographed by Marius Petipa and set to the music of Ludwig Minkus. It was first performed in St. Petersburg in Russia in 1877 and is one of Petipa's greatest ballets. Set in India, the ballet tells the tragic story of the temple dancer Nikiya's love for the warrior Solor. A scene from it, known as The Kingdom of the Shades, is one of the most famous set pieces in Classical ballet for the corps de ballet. On the left, Laura Morera performs as the evil Gamzatti. In the center, Roberta Marquez and Steven McRae perform as Nikiya and Solar. On the right, Roberta Marquez is Nikiya again.

BALLET TODAY

I N THE EARLY 20TH CENTURY, BALLET CHANGED. PEOPLE started to get tired of traditional Classical ballet and wanted to see something new. An exciting new era known as **Neoclassical ballet** began.

The Ballets Russes

The driving force behind this change was a man called Sergey Diaghilev, a Russian producer and director. Diaghilev brought together a company called the Ballets Russes that toured Europe and America with exciting new ballets that were much more expressive and dramatic than the traditional Classical ballets that had gone before.

Diaghilev brought in new composers such as Igor Stravinsky, and revolutionary artists, such as Pablo Picasso, who created innovative music, sets, and costumes for his ballets. He also signed the famous Russian ballerina, Anna Pavlova, for their first Paris season in 1909. The Ballets Russes is regarded as one of the most influential ballet companies of the 20th century because it changed things so much.

The later 20th century

As time went by, generations of new dancers and choreographers brought fresh ideas to ballet. They were less restricted and could borrow from other styles of dance, such as jazz and **contemporary dance**. One of Diaghilev's dancers, George Balanchine, became one of the most influential choreographers of the 20th century. He was a fellow Russian who later went to live in the United States, where he founded the New York City Ballet and worked on developing abstract ballet, where no story is necessary to hold the ballet together.

A poster advertizes the Ballets Russes at the Royal Opera House in 1912. Ninette de Valois, who founded The Royal Ballet, danced with the Ballets Russes for three years and helped to bring Russian ballet to Britain.

Yuhui Choe in "Rubies" from Jewels, choreographed by George Balanchine.

*Edward Watson (third from right) as The Chosen One in **The Rite of Spring**, choreographed by Kenneth MacMillan. The music for this ballet was composed by Igor Stravinsky for the Ballets Russes. Stravinsky later became a major 20th-century composer.*

RUSSIAN BALLET

ROYAL OPERA
COVENT GARDEN
· SEASON 1912 ·

SIXPENCE NET   LONDON · JOHN LONG Lᵀᴰ

Brand-new ballets

Nowadays, the traditional Romantic and Classical ballets of the 19th century are still highly popular. They appear in new versions but their charm remains the same. Alongside the traditional ballets, ballet companies perform works from throughout the different ballet eras and continually commission new ballets as well. When a new work is commissioned, it can be inspired by absolutely anything. Often everything is created from scratch, from choreography and music to costumes and scenery, which is a huge undertaking.

*Sarah Lamb and Eric Underwood in **Raven Girl**, choreographed for The Royal Ballet by Wayne McGregor. **Raven Girl** is a modern fairy tale based on a story by Audrey Niffenegger, about a girl who has the soul of a bird.*

MARGOT FONTEYN

BORN: 1919 **DIED:** 1991
NATIONALITY: British

Margot Fonteyn joined the Vic-Wells Ballet in 1934, dancing a Classical repertory and creating roles in new ballets by Frederick Ashton, including *Ondine*. She also danced in the **premiere** of Kenneth MacMillan's *Romeo and Juliet* in 1965, alongside Rudolf Nureyev, her famous dance partner. Fonteyn and Nureyev had a celebrated partnership, which started when they danced *Giselle* together in 1962 and lasted until the 1980s.

*Fonteyn and Nureyev in rehearsal for Kenneth MacMillan's production of **Romeo and Juliet**, first performed in 1965.*

RUDOLF NUREYEV

BORN: 1938 **DIED:** 1993
NATIONALITY: Russian (later taking Austrian citizenship)

Rudolf Nureyev began his career with the Kirov Ballet (now the Mariinsky Ballet) in Leningrad (now St. Petersburg) in the former Soviet Union. He was a brilliant dancer but found it difficult to conform to his country's politics, which restricted personal freedoms such as travel. On tour in Paris in 1961, he left the Kirov Ballet to seek asylum in France. By then he was well known and in 1962, Ninette de Valois invited him to dance with The Royal Ballet, where he stayed until 1970. He spent the rest of his career performing around the world, as well as continuing as a guest artist with The Royal Ballet.

*Fonteyn and Nureyev in **Marguerite and Armand**.*

ABOUT THE ·
ROYAL BALLET

THE ROYAL BALLET IS BASED AT THE ROYAL OPERA HOUSE IN Covent Garden in London, UK. Both the opera house and the ballet company have a long history, as there has been a theater on the same site since 1732.

The Royal Opera House, Covent Garden. The front of the building, the foyer, and auditorium date from 1858.

Royal Ballet beginnings

Ballet had been staged in London since the 17th century but the origins of The Royal Ballet date from the early 20th century. It all began with the British dancer Ninette de Valois. She danced with the Ballets Russes in the 1920s and was herself an exceptional dancer. She very much wanted to set up a school for British dancers, where they could be trained in a "British" style. By 1931 she had established the Vic-Wells Ballet company and school, based at Sadler's Wells Theatre in London. She recruited dancers from the Ballets Russes, including the famous British ballerina Alicia Markova.

In 1939, the company became known as Sadler's Wells Ballet and in 1946, after World War II, it was invited to move to the newly reopened Royal Opera House in London's Covent Garden, opening with a production of *The Sleeping Beauty*. A separate company remained at Sadler's Wells. Then, in 1956, a royal charter was granted and the company and the school were renamed The Royal Ballet and The Royal Ballet School. In 1990, Sadler's Wells Royal Ballet, as the touring arm of The Royal Ballet had become known, relocated to Birmingham, UK and became the Birmingham Royal Ballet. All three organizations now rank among the best in the world—a tribute to Ninette de Valois, who was the driving force behind British ballet.

*Members of The Royal Ballet corps de ballet in their dressing room at the Royal Opera House, Covent Garden. They are in costume as Stars in the 1960 revival of the 1948 Sadler's Wells Ballet production of **Cinderella**.*

Royal Opera House

There have been three theaters in Covent Garden but the theater we see today has been there since 1858; the previous two theaters were destroyed by fire. During World War Two, the theater was a dance hall but in 1946 the decision was made to make it the home of both an opera company and a ballet company—and that's how it remains today.

In 1997, the Royal Opera House was closed for two and a half years so that it could be modernized and extended. New public areas, rehearsal rooms, workrooms, and offices were added, and the whole site now covers two-and-a-half acres! Today, the Royal Opera House employs a staff of over 900 and puts on around 400 performances a year, with seating for over 2,200 people for every performance.

Signature ballet

Some companies have a signature ballet, which means a ballet that it is best known for performing and which represents it well as a company. The Royal Ballet's signature ballet is *The Sleeping Beauty*—a grand and spectacular performance with a huge cast!

The Sleeping Beauty has been part of The Royal Ballet's repertory since the early days, when it was still known as the Sadler's Wells Ballet. This poster dates from 1946, when the company moved to the Royal Opera House.

Artists of The Royal Ballet in a scene from the 2011 performance of The Sleeping Beauty.

ANTOINETTE SIBLEY

BORN: 1939   **NATIONALITY:** British

Antoinette Sibley joined The Royal Ballet from The Royal Ballet School in 1956, having danced her first role with the company earlier that year when still a student. By 1959 she was a soloist and in 1960 she was promoted to **Principal dancer**. She is also famous for her dance partnership with Anthony Dowell and for the roles created for her by choreographer Frederick Ashton, notably Titania in *The Dream* and the title role in Kenneth MacMillan's *Manon*.

ANTHONY DOWELL

BORN: 1943   **NATIONALITY:** British

Anthony Dowell was one of the greatest male dancers of the 20th century. Frederick Ashton cast him as Oberon in *The Dream*, opposite Antoinette Sibley. This was the start of their famous partnership. Together, they were known for their technical ability and their excellent awareness of music and rhythm. Anthony Dowell later became Director of The Royal Ballet, from 1986 to 2001.

Antoinette Sibley and Anthony Dowell as Titania and Oberon in Frederick Ashton's The Dream, 1964.

CHAPTER TWO

CREATING A BALLET

There are so many elements that go into performing a ballet. It's not just the dancing and the music, it's the scenery and costumes and detail that make it all work.

Opposite: Tamara Rojo and David Makhateli in a scene from a performance of Les Sylphides *in 2013, a ballet in the Romantic style from the early 20th century.*

CHOREOGRAPHY

GOING TO SEE A DANCE PERFORMANCE CAN BE A THRILLING experience. But have you ever thought about who chooses the story or theme, who creates the dance steps, and who imagines the scenery and costumes? All dance sequences, from ballet to ballroom dancing, have to be thought up by someone and this person is called the choreographer.

*Frederick Ashton, the choreographer, works out positions with Margot Fonteyn and Michael Somes for his ballet **Ondine** in 1958.*

Ballet notation

The choreographer's main job is to create the dance steps. As the steps are being arranged they are often recorded in note form, in a similar way to how musical notes are recorded on a music score. The positions of the head, arms, hands, legs, and feet are all noted down. The person who does this is called the notator, and he or she works quickly as the choreographer works out steps with the dancers.

Using notation means that there is a written record to help everyone remember the steps. Also, in this way, the choreography of a ballet can be preserved exactly so that if an old ballet is brought back to the stage, the company has a record of all the dancers' steps.

In the style of notation known as Benesh Movement Notation, the body is shown on a five-line grid, called a stave. The marks show the positions and movements of the parts of the body.

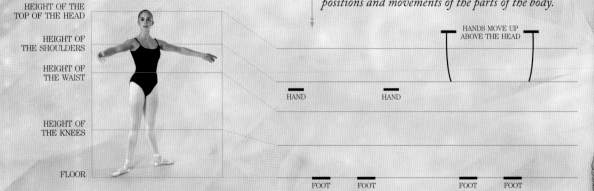

HEIGHT OF THE TOP OF THE HEAD
HEIGHT OF THE SHOULDERS
HEIGHT OF THE WAIST
HEIGHT OF THE KNEES
FLOOR

HANDS MOVE UP ABOVE THE HEAD
HAND HAND
FOOT FOOT FOOT FOOT

Some famous choreographers

❀ MARIUS PETIPA (1818–1910)
A French choreographer who created some of the great classics for the Imperial Russian Ballet, including *The Sleeping Beauty* and *Swan Lake*.

❀ FREDERICK ASHTON (1904–88)
Founder choreographer of The Royal Ballet who created what became known as the English style, including *Cinderella* and *La Fille mal gardée*.

❀ GEORGE BALANCHINE (1904–83)
Russian dancer who founded the New York City Ballet, where he was famous for producing abstract ballets. His works include *Jewels, Orpheus, Apollo,* and *Symphony in C.*

❀ JEROME ROBBINS (1918–98)
One of America's greatest dance makers and, with Balanchine, a founder choreographer of New York City Ballet. He also choreographed extensively for film, TV, and theater including, famously, *West Side Story.*

Romeo and Juliet by Kenneth MacMillan, set to music by Prokofiev. In this scene, Juliet's cousin Tybalt (Bennet Gartside), has killed Romeo's friend Mercutio.

❋ JOHN CRANKO (1927–73)
South African-born choreographer with Sadler's Wells ballet and most famously Stuttgart Ballet, of which he was also Director. He created ballets such as *Onegin*, *The Prince of the Pagodas* and *The Taming of the Shrew*.

❋ KENNETH MACMILLAN (1929–92)
Former Director of The Royal Ballet, he is known for his theatrical ballets about human nature. Among his best-known works are *Romeo and Juliet*, *Manon*, and *Mayerling*.

❋ WAYNE MCGREGOR (1970–)
He became Resident Choreographer of The Royal Ballet in 2006—the first contemporary dance maker to be given the post. He is particularly renowned for his abstract ballets.

❋ CHRISTOPHER WHEELDON (1973–)
Artistic Associate of The Royal Ballet, and formerly the first ever Resident Choreographer of New York City Ballet. He is admired both for his abstract and his story ballets, most recently *The Winter's Tale*.

Christopher Wheeldon at work.

Kristen McNally

"One of the wonderful things about being a choreographer is that there are no rules—you can discover what works for you. Inspiration can come from anywhere: people, landscape, art, science, architecture, film, music, life— and so your journey to the finished piece can be different every time. For me, it's often music that inspires me. It triggers ideas and then I work from there.

There's a comfort in having an existing piece of music that is familiar and inspires a big part of your initial thinking on a new work. However, it's unusual to find the perfect score—it'll be too long, not long enough, or you'll want a certain section to repeat and so a reorchestration is often needed. This is difficult to get permission for. Alternatively, it's amazing to have a piece of music specially commissioned and you can work side by side with the composer and create exactly what you want.

When we create a new ballet at the Royal Opera House, the designs, costumes, styling, and sets will have been done before the choreographer even gets into the studio with the dancers. There is room for tweaking and changing things along the way and the choreographer and designer will often make final decisions together. Ballets at the Royal Opera House always have the choreographer at the helm so the designer is realizing the choreographer's vision and therefore the choreographer has the final say!

Dancers can often be the inspiration for new choreography. When you start work in the studio, it's a constant partnership between dancer and choreographer.

I love being on both sides, as I am also a dancer. What I enjoy most about choreographing is being creative, experimenting with your wildest ideas to create a world for the audience to immerse themselves in!"

Kristen McNally
CHOREOGRAPHER AND SOLOIST
WITH THE ROYAL BALLET

Kristen McNally works with a group of young children at the Royal Opera House.

- ROMEO AND JULIET -

Lauren Cuthbertson as Juliet and Federico Bonelli as Romeo in a performance for The Royal Ballet in 2012 of *Romeo and Juliet*, choreographed by Kenneth MacMillan. The couple dance joyfully as they express their love in the Balcony scene in Act I.

MUSIC
- FOR THE -
BALLET

When you go to see a ballet, you also get another special treat—a live orchestra playing wonderful music! When people think of music for ballet, they often remember the great Classical pieces, such as music from *Swan Lake* or *The Nutcracker*. However, ballet can be performed to any style of music.

The orchestra

A traditional orchestra for ballet can include around one hundred musicians. They are arranged into four sections, depending on what instrument they play:

* STRING INSTRUMENTS—violin, viola, cello, double bass, piano, harp
* WIND INSTRUMENTS—flute, oboe, clarinet, bassoon
* BRASS INSTRUMENTS—horn, trumpet, trombone, tuba
* PERCUSSION INSTRUMENTS—drum, triangle, cymbal, xylophone

A view inside the Royal Opera House auditorium, showing the stage and the orchestra pit directly in front of it.

This is a typical seating chart for an orchestra. The actual seating often changes depending on what instruments are playing, the conductor's preferences, and the space available.

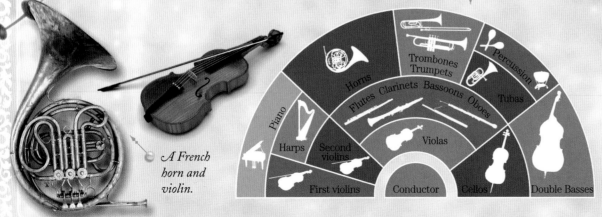

A French horn and violin.

The orchestra pit

The orchestra sits in an area directly in front of the stage, called the pit, which is sunk down below the level of the audience. The audience can see parts of the orchestra during the performance, but the dancers on the stage cannot. Usually, the string section sits at the front, nearest the audience. The wind and brass sections are in the middle, and the percussion section sits at the back.

The pit floor can be raised and lowered so that heavy instruments can be lifted up from storage below and not carried into the **auditorium**, which would be awkward.

The conductor

A conductor directs the orchestra, keeping it in time and helping it to interpret the music by moving his or her arms and hands, holding a stick called a baton. The members of the orchestra watch the conductor so that they know when to come in, when to play louder, when to speed up, and so on.

The musicians are totally reliant on the conductor to help them keep time with the dancers. The conductor will normally attend the dancers' rehearsals so that he or she can learn how the dancers are interpreting the music and the different tempos (speeds) at which they are dancing certain pieces.

In the story, Peter prevents hunters from shooting the Wolf (Sergei Polunin) and takes it to a zoo.

The Bird (Laurine Muccioli) helps to distract the Wolf, while Peter captures it.

Peter (Kilian Smith), his Grandfather (Will Kemp), and the animal characters from Peter and the Wolf.

Peter and the Wolf

In 1936, Russian composer Sergey Prokofiev created a piece of music for children based on the fairy tale *Peter and the Wolf*. The story is also narrated, as well as played by instruments. The characters in the story are represented by specific instruments, so this piece of music is often used to teach children about the orchestra. For instance, Peter is played by the string section, the Wolf is played by a French horn, and the Bird is played by a flute.

Peter and the Wolf has also been made into a ballet. In 1995, Matthew Hart choreographed the music for The Royal Ballet School and it was narrated by Anthony Dowell, then the Director of The Royal Ballet.

Barry Wordsworth

"The role of the conductor is fundamental to the success of any ballet. During a performance, he or she needs to be aware of the music and the choreography in equal measure. Conductors are trained musicians and it is essential that they know how to work as a team and mix their musical convictions with the concept of those with whom they are working.

There is not much time for the dancers to work with the orchestra, so the conductor must make sure that not a second is wasted on matters that could have been sorted out in the piano rehearsals. This is because during the performances, the orchestra must be alert to differences that occur from night to night due to changes of cast. The orchestra can hear the singers in an opera and be alert to them on stage, but in the ballet they can only rely on the conductor for subtle changes of pace and mood."

Barry Wordsworth
MUSIC DIRECTOR
OF THE ROYAL BALLET

STUNNING SETS

A model set from *Alice's Adventures in Wonderland*, showing the garden of the Queen of Hearts and a model of a ballerina.

The real scenery on stage. Tamara Rojo as The Red Queen plays croquet with a flamingo as a mallet and a hedgehog as a ball, as described in the book!

EVERY AUDIENCE WANTS TO SEE THE SKILL OF THE DANCERS— and this is set off by the way the stage is decorated to show off the performance. The whole display comes together on stage with an arrangement of scenery, called the set, which complements the dancers, their costumes, and the music.

Set design

When a choreographer begins to think about a ballet, he or she will often imagine the way the design will help the dancers show off their talent. Set designers work with the choreographer to create ideas and the dance steps themselves have a big influence on the set design. For instance, if a dancer has to look through a window, the window has to be precisely placed to allow him or her to get there in time with the music.

The actual design starts off with sketches and then progresses to models, which are made to scale. When everyone is happy with the model, a full-size set is created.

In 2011, The Royal Ballet created its first full-length ballet since 1995. Choreographed by Christopher Wheeldon and designed by Bob Crowley, its inspiration was Lewis Carroll's famous book of 1865, *Alice's Adventures in Wonderland*. One of the scenery backgrounds was the garden of the Queen of Hearts, imagined as a maze.

The whole design of the ballet reflects the crazy world that Alice finds herself in when she follows the White Rabbit into Wonderland. Here, the corps de ballet are dressed as playing cards, with their tutus made from stiff foam in the shape of hearts, diamonds, clubs, and spades.

Using props

Another important element of a ballet set are the props—these are objects that the dancers need to use when they are telling a story. These can be anything from fairy wands and goblets to tables and swords. A big ballet company performing in a large theater will need a very large collection of props. The Royal Opera House even has its own armory department where swords and weapons are made and kept especially for fight scenes.

*Nehemiah Kish as The Prince and artists of The Royal Ballet in Kenneth MacMillan's **The Prince of the Pagodas**. The dancers are specially trained to enact the fight scene to make it look realistic.*

In the limelight!

Many years ago, theater lighting used a chemical called quicklime, which glowed brightly. That's where we get the word "limelight," meaning "the center of attention." In fact, it was at Covent Garden Theatre in 1837 that quicklime was used for the first time for indoor theater lighting.

Nowadays, the correct lighting is obviously a vital part of theater staging. The auditorium is dark, so the lighting directs and focuses the audience's attention to what is happening on stage. There are different types of theater lighting for different purposes, and the people who look after them are called lighting technicians.

* SPOTLIGHTS—these are lights with narrow beams to light up a certain spot or a dancer on stage.

* FOLLOW SPOTS—these are lights that can move around the stage and follow individual dancers.

* FLOODLIGHTS—these are rows of lights in metal boxes that hang above the stage for lighting up a large area.

* FOOTLIGHTS—these are rows of lights along the floor at the front of the stage.

Here you can see the floodlights hanging above the main stage. There are also spotlights hanging from scaffolding. At the back of this picture, the auditorium is visible.

Moving scenery is heavy work—but it all has to be done on time for the curtain to go up.

Quick turnaround

During a run of performances, there may be several different productions going on—all with their own scenery, props, and lighting requirements. Sometimes there are two performances a day, so it takes a large crew of people to change the sets both during the show and also to get ready for the next one. For instance, at the Royal Opera House there are three separate crews who work over a 24-hour shift, with 25 people in each crew. To help move heavy scenery, the Royal Opera House also has the largest backstage elevator in Europe!

SPECTACULAR COSTUMES

Costumes for a ballet are designed to complement the ballet's style and also to help tell the ballet's story or theme. And, of course, they have to be comfortable to dance in—whether they are complex and richly designed or just simple leotards!

Costume design

The first thing to do when creating a costume is to draw up a design. The choreographer will have an opinion on how he or she wants the costume to look, then the designer will do sketches and suggest materials. The designer and the costume department then have to work out how much a costume will cost to make. Sometimes a design has to be adapted to fall within the budget. Once the costume materials have been agreed upon, they can be ordered and the costumes are made and fitted to the dancers.

A costume design by Ian Spurling for The Royal Ballet's Elite Syncopations choreographed by Kenneth MacMillan to music by Scott Joplin and others. Here, you can see how the original design transformed into the actual costume worn by Mara Galeazzi.

Some costumes are very elaborate, especially for those who perform character roles. This costume belongs to Kostcheï in The Firebird, here danced by Gary Avis, and helps to illustrate his role as a fearful magician.

David Pickering as The Mouse King in The Royal Ballet's 2009 performance of The Nutcracker. The dancer wears a typical male costume—tights, ballet boots, and a jacket—but the look is completed with an elaborate mask and a tail.

Work, work, work!

A large ballet company's costume department usually has a heavy workload. There might be two or three productions happening during any one period and all the costumes have to be either made or adapted beforehand. They might also need to be repaired if they get damaged during the performances—sometimes as an emergency on the side of the stage!

Many of the costumes have very fine detail, such as this jeweled headdress. The pieces are all stitched or stuck on by hand.

A costume being made in the costume workroom at the Royal Opera House.

This design has fabric swatches stuck to it, as a record of the exact materials used.

At the Royal Opera House, which creates costumes for both ballet and opera, the costume department has to look after thousands of costumes. In a recent ballet season, for instance, the department had to remake 36 skirts for the Snowflakes in *The Nutcracker*, making just one a day! At the same time, the team had to adjust all the costumes for *Onegin*, plus 40 dresses for the Swans in *Swan Lake*. Then the costumes have to be fitted to the dancers—just one fitting can sometimes take up to two hours.

Costume bible

Every ballet has a book called a costume bible, which records all the costume details, including the designer's sketches, the final designs, and the exact materials used. This is so that if the ballet is ever brought back to the stage and the costumes need remaking, all the information is ready and waiting for the costume department to use.

Fay Fullerton

"I studied at the London College of Fashion taking a three-year course in Fashion, with an extra year in Period Costume and Tailoring. I then became a junior costumier at the Royal Opera House and worked my way up, becoming Head of Costume in 2013.

From day to day, I am responsible for a large creative team including dyers, ladies' and mens' costumiers, tailors, milliners (hat makers), jewelers, stockroom managers, wig and makeup technicians, costume supervisors, costume buyers, shoe technicians, costume-hire and storage technicians, and performance support technicians working on shows for both The Royal Ballet and The Royal Opera. We work closely with designers to bring their concepts to life, while working within tight budgets.

One of our most challenging productions is *The Sleeping Beauty*, as it has over 450 costumes. The skills of creating costumes for such a large ballet include sourcing large quantities of specialist fabrics that are both practical for the dancers to work in but are hardwearing enough to last the number of performances.

To make sure everything runs smoothly, I normally attend final dress rehearsals and all first nights. And each show has a team of costume, wig, and makeup technicians to deal with costume emergencies!"

Fay Fullerton
HEAD OF COSTUME

*Oliver Messel's wonderful designs for this 2011 performance of **The Sleeping Beauty** were originally created in 1946.*

- GISELLE -

Marianela Nuñez as Giselle in Peter Wright's production for The Royal Ballet. This scene from Act I shows Giselle with Count Albrecht's fiancée, Bathilde, performed by Christina Arestis.

THE TUTU

I F YOU ASK PEOPLE WHAT BALLERINAS WEAR, MOST WILL answer "A tutu"! The tutu is the most familiar ballet costume and is what every young dancer dreams of wearing. It is often decorated with lavish detail, such as embroidery, jewels, or sequins. Like all costumes it is designed to represent the character or theme that she is playing.

Sarah Lamb wears a Classical tutu in Christopher Wheeldon's **Electric Counterpoint**. *The costume was designed by Jean-Marc Puissant to create a simple, modern, but striking look.*

Bodice

Skirt

The wardrobe department at The Royal Opera House stitches on thousands of sequins and bijoux every year.

What's in a tutu?

A tutu is a layered skirt attached to a bodice. It is made in two parts: the bodice and a frilled skirt. The skirt consists of many layers of netting and can be made in different shapes, according to the style of the ballet and how the costume designer wants the tutu to look. There are two main types of tutu:

※ THE CLASSICAL TUTU sticks straight out from the dancer's hips and consists of up to 15 layers of stiff netting, supported by a wire hoop.

※ THE ROMANTIC TUTU echoes the style that was worn by ballerinas in the Romantic era of the early 19th century. It has a skirt that falls down to mid-calf or ankle length. It is long and flowing, made of up to six layers.

For practice and ordinary rehearsals, dancers wear a practice tutu so that the proper performance tutu doesn't get damaged. A professional practice tutu can be long or short depending on the role, but is usually just a skirt witout a bodice. Practice tutus move and feel like real tutus, so that the dancers feel like they are wearing their actual costumes. They won't rehearse in their real tutus until the dress rehearsal.

The designs for this ballet from the 1950s, **Birthday Offering**, show a tutu that is halfway between a Classical and a Romantic tutu.

A Classical tutu.

Natalia Osipova as Giselle in a Romantic tutu.

Show off!

A tutu is fitted snugly to the dancer's individual body shape so it shows off the way she moves. However, it can't be so tight that it's uncomfortable and restricts her. She needs to be able to move and bend freely—and sometimes wear it for a whole ballet, which could last several hours! Many Classical ballets use the Classical tutu because it reveals the whole of the dancer's legs and feet so the audience can appreciate her skill.

The costume department

Tutus are works of art and a huge amount of effort goes into making them. The costume department at the Royal Opera House is responsible for making and looking after all of the costumes, including the tutus. Not only do the tutus have to look beautiful, they also have to be strong so that they last—a tutu might be worn up to 40 times in one season!

The costume department makes or adapts the tutus from the designer's sketches. Each tutu then has to be fitted to the dancer—or adjusted so that it can be made to fit several dancers. The costume makers do their best to make sure that each dancer is comfortable and that there are no bits that irritate. It is an enormous amount of work to do this for a whole production—for instance, in a big ballet such as *The Sleeping Beauty*, there could be over 450 different costumes.

Making a tutu in the costume department of the Royal Opera House.

- BEAUTIFUL BALLET -
SHOES

PUTTING ON YOUR FIRST PAIR OF BALLET SHOES IS A VERY exciting moment! If you do ballet, you'll know that you start off wearing leather or satin ballet flats. Professional dancers, however, wear different types of shoes depending on the roles they are playing.

Ballet flats

At first, girls wear pink ballet flats and boys wear black ones for practice. These have flat soles to show the shape of the foot. They have ribbon or elastic ties, with a drawstring at the front for tightening them. It's a good idea to keep your shoes tidy by tucking the ribbons and elastics in when you've finished dancing. You could also keep your shoes in a bag to keep them clean.

A dancer wearing ballet flats and leg warmers for practice. You can see the round toes and flat soles of the shoes.

The role of Bottom in **The Dream** *is danced on pointe by Jonathan Howells for comic effect.*

Broken-down pointe shoes, after they have been worn in and used several times.

The correct position for dancing on pointe is shown here. The tip of the shoe must be flat on the floor, with the box at right angles to the floor.

Dancing on pointe

When girls are ready to progress, their teacher might suggest that they start dancing on pointe. **Pointe shoes** allow a dancer to balance on the tips of her toes for long periods of time, making her look elegant, as if she were floating. This is because pointe shoes make the foot look longer, like an extension of the leg. Pointe shoes are normally worn only by female dancers but some male roles require them, such as the character of Bottom in *The Dream*.

All dancers have different-shaped feet, so manufacturers make shoes in different models to fit. At the very tip of the shoe is a section called the box, which is a hard case with a flat end that supports the dancer's toes. The box is made of several layers of burlap (a coarse cloth) and canvas, each stiffened in glue. The rest of the shoe has a stiffened sole to support the arch of the foot. The shoes are then covered in satin.

Pointe shoes are very stiff and some dancers prefer to wear them once they have been softened. To do this they sometimes bang them on a hard surface such as the floor; this also makes them less noisy. When they become too soft, dancers sometimes re-stiffen them with a resin called shellac. Pointe shoes don't last very long—sometimes only a couple of shows—so professional dancers go through a lot of shoes.

Character shoes and boots

Not all roles require ballet flats or pointe shoes. Men sometimes wear ballet boots—these are like flat ballet shoes, but with a boot rising up the leg. Men and women may also wear character boots or shoes, which have heels.

La Fille mal gardée, a ballet by Frederick Ashton that received its premiere in 1960, contains a famous clog dance. This picture shows Philip Mosley as Widow Simone, leading the dance.

*The Stepsisters from **Cinderella** are men dressed as women (here Alastair Marriott and Jonathan Howells). They wear character shoes to dance in.*

The shoe department

Each year, The Royal Ballet's dancers get through 6,000 pairs of ballet flats and 6,000 pairs of pointe shoes! The shoe department looks after the shoes, making sure that each dancer has enough pairs to keep him or her going through rehearsals and performances. The shoes are kept in pigeonholes, marked with the dancers' names, so they can help themselves to another pair when they need to.

The shoe department is also responsible for dyeing and decorating shoes to match the costumes. For instance, for the blue shoes worn by the Caterpillar in *Alice's Adventures in Wonderland*, 365 crystals are applied on to each shoe.

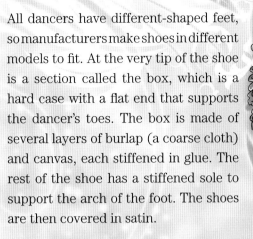

The Caterpillar is danced by eight dancers, so there are 16 legs and 16 shoes exactly like this!

Pigeonholes for the dancers' shoes.

HAIR
– AND –
MAKEUP

AN IMPORTANT PART OF ANY DANCER'S LOOK IS THEIR HAIR and makeup. Their faces have to be seen by the audience from afar, as facial expressions are important in putting across the emotion of the performance.

Claire Calvert, soloist with The Royal Ballet, in full makeup with exaggerated dark eyes and lips.

Changing faces

All dancers wear makeup on stage in order to define their eyes, lips, and cheekbones so that they can be seen clearly by the audience. They use products specifically designed for the stage so they last right through the performance and are waterproof so they don't wash away when the dancer is sweating. Greasepaint is still used for creating big character makeups as it blends easily, but it's important to set it with powder as otherwise it will smear and come off on the dancers' costumes.

Tristan Dyer puts his makeup on before a performance.

Matching wigs ensure that all the dancers have the same hairstyle and headdress, if necessary.

Pretty hair—and fantastic wigs!

Ballerinas traditionally have their hair up and away from their face. Many roles require a headdress—and some require a wig, especially if all the dancers have to have the same color and style of hair. Wigs may also have decoration attached, or tiaras or crowns.

Elsa Godard backstage at the Royal Opera House puts the finishing touches to her hair and headdress in the dressing room before putting on her costume.

Lynn Seymour in A Month in the Country, 1976.

David Wall as Petrucchio in The Taming of the Shrew, 1977.

LYNN SEYMOUR

BORN: 1939   **NATIONALITY:** Canadian

Lynn Seymour was one of the greatest dance actresses of her generation, and was a Principal with The Royal Ballet from 1959 to 1966, and then a Guest Principal from 1971 to 1978. She was celebrated for her technical and dramatic powers, and two of The Royal Ballet's great choreographers, Frederick Ashton and Kenneth MacMillan, created some of their most dramatic roles for her. These include Ashton's Natalia Petrovna in *A Month in the Country* and the wonderful barefoot solo *Five Brahms Waltzes in the Manner of Isadora Duncan*. MacMillan created Mary Vetsera in *Mayerling* and Juliet in *Romeo and Juliet* for her, and it is these ballets for which she is most renowned.

DAVID WALL

BORN: 1946   **DIED:** 2013

NATIONALITY: British

In 1966, at the age of just 21, David Wall became The Royal Ballet's youngest-ever male Principal. He had an amazing stage presence that opened up new dramatic possibilities for the great choreographers of the day. His partners included leading ballerinas such as Lynn Seymour and Margot Fonteyn. One of the roles created for him was Crown Prince Rudolf in Kenneth MacMillan's ballet *Mayerling*. The role is still regarded as the most emotionally demanding and physically challenging Principal male role of all. Wall's stunning **jeté** is immortalized in the 1975 bronze statue by Enzo Plazzotta that can be seen on London's Chelsea Embankment.

39

CHAPTER THREE

LIFE IN A
BALLET
COMPANY

A ballet company is a busy place of work. It doesn't just include the dancers—teams of people behind the scenes work to create the ballet, make costumes and scenery and, of course, sell tickets to the show!

Opposite: An artist from the Sadler's Wells Theatre Ballet waits in the wings during the production of Assembly Ball in 1946.

DIRECTING
- A BALLET COMPANY -

THE MOST IMPORTANT PERSON BEHIND THE SCENES IS the Director of the company. All companies need to have someone in charge who makes the big decisions and tells everyone what to do.

Being the Director

The main roles of the Director of a ballet company are to decide how the company operates, what ballets to perform, and who dances which parts. The Director oversees each production. He or she works with all the members of the team to make sure that everyone delivers their best work, down to the finest detail. People who become Directors were often Principal dancers themselves, so they know all about the demands of delivering a perfect performance and what it takes to be the best.

Sometimes the Director may rehearse individual dancers to make sure that they are conveying their roles in the way that the Director wants. The art of ballet is all about communicating with the audience. It would be no good dancing perfect steps if there were no emotional connection: that is, if the audience doesn't care about the characters or the story or what they are seeing on stage. It's the Director's job to make sure this connection happens.

Ninette de Valois

The founder of The Royal Ballet and its very first Director, Ninette de Valois is regarded as one of the most influential people in the history of ballet. Born in Ireland in 1898, she moved to England when she was seven and started studying ballet at age 13. By the age of 21, she was dancing professionally in operas at Covent Garden. In 1923, she joined the Ballets Russes. She was also a mentor (teacher and supporter) to Alicia Markova, who became one of the best British dancers ever.

De Valois became utterly determined to found a school for British dancers and run her own company. The school and company began at Sadler's Wells and later transformed into The Royal Ballet School, The Royal Ballet and Birmingham Royal Ballet (see pages 18–19). She was Director of The Royal Ballet until 1963, when she retired to concentrate on The Royal Ballet School, but she continued to be involved in ballet for the rest of her life. She died in 2001 at the age of 102.

Ninette de Valois, Founder Director of The Royal Ballet.

Kevin O'Hare, appointed as Director of The Royal Ballet in 2012.

Ballet on tour

National and international touring is part of almost every ballet company's life. Where the company tours is the decision of the Director, after discussion with the technical teams.

To begin with, the team must visit venues to check the size and facilities of the possible theaters, including nearby rehearsal space and suitable accommodation. This will happen perhaps a year or more in advance of the tour. Costumes and sets then travel to the venue by ship or truck a couple of months in advance.

Tours involve an enormous amount of planning and organization, especially if the venue is overseas, but it is a fantastic opportunity for a company to bring their peformances to a much wider audience of ballet lovers. It's also a wonderful experience for all the dancers involved.

The Royal Ballet on tour in Tokyo, Japan, 2013.

More people behind the scenes

Apart from performing, there are many other roles that are essential to running a ballet company. Here are some of them:

❉ BALLET MASTER OR MISTRESS
Takes the dancers through their rehearsals and teaches them their roles in the different ballets.

❉ REPETITEUR
Rehearses the dancers, often the Principals and Soloists, in specific ballets.

❉ BALLET TEACHER
Takes the dancers through their daily **class** (practice session).

❉ SCHEDULER
Coordinates the daily rehearsal schedule and rehearsal and performance casting.

❉ NOTATOR
Records the steps of new ballets as the choreographer works them out, and sees that existing ballets are revived accurately from the notation score.

❉ PIANIST
Plays for the dancers' daily classes and rehearsals and sometimes in performance with the orchestra.

❉ HEALTHCARE TEAM
Looks after the health and well-being of the dancers (*see pages 48-49*).

❉ STAGE MANAGER
Ensures the smooth technical running of each performance and that everything happens at the right time.

❉ HAIR AND MAKEUP ARTIST
Helps the dancers apply their makeup and hair, especially any complex or special effects when necessary.

❉ WARDROBE STAFF
Specialist staff who look after wigs, costumes, and shoes.

❉ DRESSER
Helps to get the dancers ready in their costumes for their performance.

- SWAN LAKE -

Sarah Lamb and Federico Bonelli dance the principal roles of Prince Siegfried and Odette in *Swan Lake*, 2011, with the corps de ballet as the Swans. Prince Siegfried has fallen in love with Odette, but she is under a curse and exists as a swan during the daytime, only becoming human at night.

BELONGING TO A
BALLET COMPANY

The Royal Ballet's Marianela Nuñez practices for her performance in the rehearsal studio, while the other cast members look on.

A BALLET COMPANY'S JOB IS TO CREATE AND PERFORM ballets for their audiences. Companies normally have a home theater, where they do most of their performing. They also often go on tour, which means that they travel to different cities and even different countries to perform their shows.

The repertory

Every ballet company has a repertory, which means a set of ballets that they know and regularly perform. From time to time, a company might introduce a new ballet to its repertory, which could either be something that is newly composed or an older ballet that it wants to bring back to the stage.

In one season, which for The Royal Ballet is a year, the company might expect to perform perhaps six full-length ballets, plus five mixed bills. It may perform several times a week and also in the afternoon on certain days. Afternoon performances are called matinees.

Famous ballet companies

THE ROYAL BALLET
❋

Based at the Royal Opera House in London, UK, The Royal Ballet was founded by Ninette de Valois in 1931, as the Vic-Wells Ballet. It is now Britain's largest ballet company.

BIRMINGHAM ROYAL BALLET
❋

Previously Sadler's Wells Royal Ballet, which was to become the touring arm of The Royal Ballet. It moved to Birmingham, UK and changed its name in 1990 and became an independent company in 1997.

THE BOLSHOI BALLET
❋

The Bolshoi Ballet in Moscow, Russia, has been performing with that name since 1825. It developed the "Moscow style," influenced by Russian folklore.

THE MARIINSKY BALLET
❋

This famous company based in St. Petersburg in Russia can trace its roots to the 1730s, and was for a time called the Kirov Ballet. It is known for its Classical style.

PARIS OPÉRA BALLET
❋

This is the oldest ballet company in the world, having been in existence since the 17th century. It performs at the Palais Garnier Opera House in Paris.

A dancer's day

A dancer's life is a very busy one! Here, two Royal Ballet dancers,
Yasmine Naghdi and Marcelino Sambé, explain how they spend a typical day.

"YASMINE: I arrive at the Royal Opera House around 9:30 a.m. First, I go to my dressing room, change into a leotard, arrange my hair, wrap myself in warm-up clothes, and organize my ballet bag with all the things I need, such as pointe shoes, snacks, fruit, and drinks. Then, I warm up before the start of our ballet class. Class usually lasts for an hour and a quarter.

MARCELINO: Class is what prepares you for the day. We start with exercises at the **barre**, where we warm our feet and calves. After this, we start a series of barre exercises that progress in difficulty. We start with the basic **demi plié** (a soft bend of the knees in four different positions) and progress to the vigorous grand battement (a big controlled throw of the leg back to the initial position).

YASMINE: We are then ready for a day of rehearsals for upcoming ballets and the evening performance. We also have costume, wig, and shoe fittings, physiotherapy, massage sessions, and extra strength-training. If my rehearsal schedule allows me free time I rest, chat with my colleagues, or sew ribbons on my pointe shoes.

MARCELINO: Between the morning class and the first rehearsals we get a short break, when I usually change my clothes, which are really sweaty after the ballet class. For lunch we get an hour, which I spend with my friends chatting and stretching in our rest area. After that we keep rehearsing until the day is finished.

YASMINE: We finish rehearsing at 5:30 p.m. so that we can rest before the evening performance. I eat an energy-boosting meal, warm up again, put on my makeup and costume, and mentally prepare. If I am dancing a solo, I visualize my performance just before I go on stage.

MARCELINO: When we don't have a performance, we usually finish at 6:30 p.m., which gives me time to go home and spend some time with my friends. Talking with my family by Skype makes me feel relaxed and of course a nice bath always does the trick! But on performance nights we usually finish at 10:30 p.m.

YASMINE: After a performance, I take off my makeup, hang up my costume, shower, and I am ready to go home around 10:50 p.m. Audience members often wait by the stage door to meet the dancers, so I spend time with them before leaving. There are many favorite moments of the day, but the best is when I come off the stage and feel I have done what I'd set out to achieve: dancing my solo to absolute perfection and hearing the audience's applause!

MARCELINO: Every morning when I wake up I feel fortunate to know that I'll spend my day doing what I really have a passion for—dancing. If I had to pick a favorite moment, I would say the curtain calls at the end of evening show, where the audience cheers and claps for our hard work. For an instant, all the fatigue of the day disappears!"

Yasmine Naghdi, First Artist and *Marcelino Sambé*, Artist

NEW YORK CITY BALLET
❃

Founded in 1948 by George Balanchine and Lincoln Kirstein. Balanchine was Director (Ballet Master in Chief) with the company until he died in 1983.

AMERICAN BALLET THEATRE
❃

Founded in 1940, this ballet company prides itself on its vast repertory. From 1980 to 1990, its artistic director was Mikhail Baryshnikov, a great dancer of the modern era.

STUTTGART BALLET
❃

Stuttgart, Germany has been a center for ballet for hundreds of years, going back to court ballet. In the 1960s, famous choreographer John Cranko founded the modern company.

– DANCERS' –
FITNESS

Whether it is dancing, football, swimming or marathon running, all top athletes need a team of people to help them keep in tip-top condition so that they are fit enough to fulfill their potential and recover quickly from injury. But, unlike many other athletes, dancers have to be at their peak fitness every single day, since in a big company they might be rehearsing four or five different ballets a week with performances on top of that. It's incredibly exciting but it's very hard work!

Tierney Heap exercises in the health-care suite.

The Royal Ballet Health Team

All ballet companies have people behind the scenes who manage dancers' fitness and injuries and keep records of each dancer's progress. The Royal Ballet has the most advanced health-care suite in the dancing world and a whole team of specialists to run it. Here is what they all do.

CLINICAL DIRECTOR
❀

He or she is in charge of managing the whole health team to ensure there is a seamless approach to managing injured dancers.

SPORTS SCIENTISTS
❀

They devise strength and fitness programs to make sure that dancers are strong and able to tolerate jumping, and that they protect their joints and reduce the risk of injury. The programs might involve lifting weights as well as general fitness and balance training.

PHYSIOTHERAPISTS
❀

They work with injured dancers to decide what the best course of action is to keep a dancer dancing or return him or her to the stage. Should an injury occur in a performance, a physiotherapist is on call to rush to the theater to assess the problem.

SOFT TISSUE THERAPISTS
❀

These specialist therapists treat problems to do with muscles, ligaments, tendons, and fascia (that's the very important tissue that surrounds your muscles), and they use special techniques and massage to help heal any injuries.

Mara Galeazzi stretches in the studio.

SPORTS AND MEDICINE DOCTOR

❉

This is a special doctor who dancers would consult if they had an injury that needed hospital treatment. All top athletes are seen in the hospital by doctors who specialize in sports medicine.

PSYCHOLOGIST

❉

Dancers have to be mentally strong to be ready to perform at their very best every night. A dance psychologist knows the special demands made on dancers and helps them keep focused, patient, and believing in themselves, especially when injured.

PILATES AND GYROTONIC INSTRUCTORS

❉

They help dancers with their flexibility and movement control using special machines, so that an injured dancer can safely return to full movement.

NUTRITIONISTS

❉

Eating healthily and regularly is really important for dancers, since they need lots of fuel to keep them going all day and give them enough energy for their performances! Nutritionists advise on the best balance of foods for dancers to eat.

REHABILITATION COACHES

❉

Often former dancers themselves, they help those returning from injury by putting all the hard work in the gym into a dance context. They consult with both the health team and the artistic staff to decide if a dancer is fully ready to perform again.

Stretching on a pilates reformer.

Recovering from injury

As one of the most gifted ballerinas of her generation, Lauren Cuthbertson found herself making her debut in big solos at quite a young age. But just as she was promoted to Principal she sprained her foot and not long afterwards she was struck with glandular fever, followed by a serious fatigue illness. While her recovery took time, it was an important learning process too.

"Dealing with minor strains and injury is part of the daily working life of a dancer but when you have a serious illness or injury, it's very hard emotionally and physically because you feel that everything you've worked so hard for disappears.

Once you have patiently allowed your body to heal you start to feel and think differently and begin to understand your body more. So when you start to rehabilitate there are many things you can improve, especially with the added benefits of a great support team. Injury makes you fight and makes you stronger but it's very hard to see this when you are feeling so frustrated and anxious at the time."

Lauren Cuthbertson,
PRINCIPAL DANCER

INSIDE THE
THEATER

As part of the audience, you only get to see a tiny part of the actual theater. Just before the show, you enter the foyer and might visit the restaurant, then the excitement builds and the bell rings to signal the start of the performance. You take your seat and the lights dim… but what else is inside the theater that you don't always get to see?

Melissa Hamilton and Gary Avis in a rehearsal studio at the Royal Opera House, showing the London skyline.

The stage

During a performance, the audience spends most of the time looking at the stage. But there's a lot more to the stage than the audience can see from the auditorium. To the left and right of the stage are areas called the **wings**, which are hidden from view. The dancers wait in the wings before they get their cue to go on stage. They also use this area to warm up before the performance.

At the back of the stage is an area where scenery can be hoisted up and down or moved in from the sides. Backstage crew work during the performance to change the scenery as the show progresses. In a large theater, the backstage area can be quite a big space, also used for assembling the sets and lighting.

An Artist from The Royal Ballet waits in the wings to go on stage.

Rehearse, rehearse, rehearse

It's easy to imagine that a theater is a very quiet place when there is no performance going on. However, that's not true—there is always something happening! For instance, two important parts of a dancer's day are class (daily training) and rehearsals. These activities normally take place in special rehearsal studios that are fitted with mirrors and barres (wooden rails for holding onto during practice). A lot of hard work is needed before the dancers are ready to perform, with perhaps three weeks of rehearsals to get through before a ballet is ready to go on.

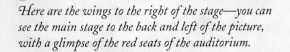

Here are the wings to the right of the stage—you can see the main stage to the back and left of the picture, with a glimpse of the red seats of the auditorium.

All in one place

When the Royal Opera House was redeveloped in the 1990s, all the facilities that The Royal Opera and The Royal Ballet needed were incorporated into the new building. This included new public areas, workrooms, offices, and rehearsal studios. Some of the rehearsal studios are exactly the same dimensions as the main stage so that the dancers can become totally familiar with the real space they have to dance in. And the best thing is they don't have to cross the city from one area to another—they can take class, relax, rehearse, and perform all in one building.

Name on the door!

Another area that the audience doesn't see is the dancers' dressing rooms. These are private areas where the dancers not only get ready for the show but also spend time if they want to relax or perhaps catch up on preparing for their role. Members of the corps de ballet will often share a dressing room but the leading performers will only share with one or two others. Dancers can personalize their space so it becomes their "home" while they are at work.

Royal Ballet Principal Thiago Soares stretching in his dressing room.

An artist's impression of the front of the Royal Opera House, when it was under reconstruction in the 1990s.

The wig workrooms at the Royal Opera House.

Front of house

The term "front of house" refers to all the parts of the theater that the audience does get to see—the foyer areas, checkrooms, restaurants, and the auditorium. People who look after these areas, such as ushers and people who sell programs and tickets, are called front-of-house staff. They spend much of the day preparing for the audience to make sure that everything is ready. All in all, a theater is a very busy place!

Part of the public area of the Royal Opera House.

CHAPTER FOUR

BALLET SCHOOL

Have you ever wondered what it would be like to go to ballet school? It's hard work but very rewarding, especially when you step onto the stage for the first time as a ballet dancer!

LEARNING BALLET

Y OU CAN START LEARNING BALLET FROM A VERY YOUNG AGE. However, if you want to become a professional ballet dancer, you have to start training seriously by the age of 11 or 12 and you will need to attend a ballet school.

Finding a class

If you want to start learning ballet, the best thing to do is to join a local school. A typical class may be for an hour or so once a week with a qualified ballet teacher. He or she will teach you steps and positions, which then build up into learning dances for performances with your classmates. Your ballet teacher will also prepare you to take exams in ballet, so that you can measure your progress and show that you have achieved certain standards.

A ballet teacher corrects a student's foot position to make sure it is pointed properly.

Going to ballet school

If you are passionate about ballet and show a lot of potential, your ballet teacher might recommend that you try to get a place at a specialist ballet school. This is usually a boarding school, where you live and study. You will learn normal academic subjects like at any school, but you will also be trained in Classical ballet at the same time. You will stay at the school until you are 16 or 18, depending on how far you take your ballet training.

To get a place at ballet school you have to **audition**, usually at age 11. An audition is a trial performance done in front of an examiner to show your skills. You might be asked to do combinations of steps to music to show your natural ability. You might also be asked to dance in a certain style or to learn and perform a short routine. The best auditions will win a place at the school!

Children can start learning ballet as young as four or five years old.

Wearing the kit!

When you are learning ballet, either at a local class or at a ballet school, you will need to wear the correct uniform. For girls, this is usually a leotard and tights with ballet flats for practice, until you are ready to move on to pointe shoes. You may also need to wear a practice skirt. When you begin to learn certain roles, you might need to wear a practice tutu. You will also have to tie back your hair or put it up in a bun. Boys normally wear a T-shirt or leotard with boy's tights, white socks, and ballet flats.

◦ *A girl has a tutu fitted at a dance store.*

◦ *A boys' ballet uniform.*

◦ *A ballet student in leotard, tights, and ballet flats, with a practice skirt.*

The life of a ballet student

"We wake up at 7:00 a.m. and have breakfast before classes start at 8:30 a.m. We have two hours of academic studies, two hours of ballet, then lunch. Then we do two more hours of academic lessons, then take a break, when we have a drink and snack and get ready for our next dance class or relax.

For our next dance classes we will do something different, such as pointe or choreographic work, or the younger years will do Scottish and Irish dancing. For our school lessons we do normal subjects such as English, math, and science, but we also do dance studies and expressive arts.

I live in a boarding house at school full-time. Each grade is kept together in one house, but girls and boys live separately. I'm with 12 other girls in rooms of two so I get to share with my best friend. I stay in regular contact with my family though and I go home every fortnight. My favorite time of day is the after-school dance class because it's relaxed and we can be more expressive.

We often perform in school productions and, at the end of the school year, we all take part in a series of summer performances at the Royal Opera House. We also perform in The Royal Ballet's Christmas productions, such as *Swan Lake* and *The Nutcracker*. Performing on stage reminds us what we're working toward. I love it—when I first did it I found it nerve-racking but once you build your confidence it becomes really fun and you just want to do the best you can.

The most exciting thing I've done so far is the Grand Defilé—the finale of our end-of-season performance on the main stage at the Royal Opera House. It's when the whole school dances onto the stage year by year. There is something special about everyone coming together; you can see the progression of technical ability through the different year groups. It makes you realize anything is possible if you work hard."

Natalia Dwyer
14-YEAR-OLD STUDENT AT THE ROYAL BALLET SCHOOL

BASIC BALLET

I N BALLET, THERE ARE BASIC POSITIONS OF THE ARMS AND FEET that most steps start and finish with. Learning the basics correctly at the beginning of your training will help you to become a confident dancer who moves with elegance, feeling, and grace.

Pointing your feet

One of the first things to learn when starting ballet is to point your feet. There should be a straight line from your hip, through your knee and ankle to your middle toe. Your foot should be stretched and elegant, making your leg look longer.

FIRST POSITION
Both arms held up in front in an oval shape.

SECOND POSITION
Arms open wide, in front of shoulders and slightly rounded.

The five positions

In ballet, there are five basic positions of the arms and feet. The positions of the arms and feet can be combined in different ways, for instance your arms can be in first while your feet are in second. However, each position is always performed exactly as shown.

FIRST POSITION
Heels touching, both feet turned out to the side.

SECOND POSITION
As in first position, but feet placed apart.

THIRD POSITION
One foot crossed halfway in front of the other.

FOURTH POSITION
One foot in front of the other with a space between them. This position can be open (with legs uncrossed) or crossed as shown here.

FIFTH POSITION
Feet are fully crossed and touching each other.

THIRD POSITION
One arm curved in front with the other out to the side.

FOURTH POSITION
One arm held up slightly in front, with the other arm out to the side and slightly rounded.

FIFTH POSITION
Both arms up in an oval shape.

Ballet moves

As you progress there are lots of ballet steps and positions to learn, a few of which are described below. Many ballet terms come from the French language because France is where the steps were first developed. All ballet moves should be performed gracefully, as if they are effortless.

✽ ARABESQUE—a position in which the dancer stands on one leg with one leg stretched out elegantly behind.

✽ BATTEMENT—a set of movements where one leg opens and closes.

✽ ENTRECHAT—a jump during which the dancer crosses her legs a number of times.

✽ GLISSADE—a gliding step.

✽ JETÉ—a springing jump off one foot and landing on another.

✽ PAS DE CHAT—a jump from one foot to the other in which the legs are drawn up to form a diamond shape.

✽ PAS DE DEUX—a dance for two.

✽ PIROUETTE—a turning step.

✽ PLIÉ—a movement in which the dancer bends her knees with her legs turned out.

✽ RELEVÉ—a movement in which the dancer rises to her toes from a flat foot.

✽ ROND DE JAMBE—a circular movement of the leg, either on the ground or in the air.

✽ SISSONNE—a scissor-like jump from two feet onto one foot.

Miming

In story ballets, the technique of mime is very important especially in the early Romantic ballets. Mime is what you do when you make a gesture to help tell the story. There are specific gestures that ballet dancers have to learn to make it clear to the audience what is happening. For instance, to mime "please," a dancer will clasp his hands in front of them or to mime "marriage," he or she will point to their ring finger.

Carlos Acosta mimes "I swear I love you" by pointing two fingers and covering his heart with the other hand.

*Federico Bonelli in **Diana and Actaeon**, performing a grand jeté.*

*Lauren Cuthbertson performs an arabesque in the role of the Fairy Godmother in **Cinderella**.*

- TIME TO RELAX -

While all professional dancers will have trained for many years to get their place in a ballet company, it is important to recharge and refresh when possible. Here, Royal Ballet Soloist Elizabeth Harrod relaxes during rehearsals.

BECOMING A BALLERINA

After a dancer has completed all the training at ballet school, the next thing is to find a job. Ballet schools are often associated with ballet companies, so that students have a natural progression from school to a company. For instance, The Royal Ballet School has an association with The Royal Ballet. However, you still have to audition to get a position.

The big moment!

A large part of a performer's life is auditioning. You will have to audition to get a job in a company but you may sometimes have to audition for a specific role in a ballet. Unfortunately, you may not always be successful as another dancer may be more suited to the part. But when you do get accepted for a role, it's a wonderful feeling of achievement. Then all you have to do is make a success of it!

Moving through the ranks

When you leave ballet school and join a company, you become a member of the corps de ballet. These dancers perform all the big ensemble dances in the ballets. Depending on your talent and experience, you will then be promoted so that you can dance solos and eventually you might become a Principal dancer, taking the lead roles.

Different ballet companies have different titles for their ranks but in The Royal Ballet, they are as follows:

❅ ARTISTS—the corps de ballet
❅ FIRST ARTISTS—the most experienced members of the corps de ballet
❅ SOLOISTS—who dance solos
❅ FIRST SOLOISTS—who dance the lead solos
❅ PRINCIPAL CHARACTER ARTISTS—who dance the character roles, where there is an emphasis on acting, as well as dancing
❅ PRINCIPALS—who dance the lead roles

The corps de ballet in "Diamonds" from George Balanchine's ballet Jewels.

A ballerina's tools— pointe shoes and a tutu!

SYLVIE GUILLEM

BORN: 1965   **NATIONALITY:** French

As a child Sylvie Guillem, originally from Paris, trained as a gymnast but was then persuaded to try ballet. At first she hated it but then found she had a love of performing. At 11 she trained at the Paris Opéra Ballet School and became the top-ranking Principal at The Paris Opéra Ballet from 1984 to 1989. She then joined The Royal Ballet as Principal Guest Artist dancing many star roles, and also danced freelance for top ballet companies. Known for her amazing technique and stage presence, she now concentrates on contemporary dance.

Sylvie Guillem standing on pointe on one leg.

IREK MUKHAMEDOV

BORN: 1960   **NATIONALITY:** Russian

Irek Mukhamedov trained at the Moscow Choreographic Institute and then danced for the touring Classical Ballet Company. In 1981 he was invited to join the Bolshoi Ballet, where he gained a reputation as a strong and muscular dancer, becoming the youngest ever to perform the role of Spartacus in the Bolshoi's signature ballet of the same name. In 1990, he left Russia to join The Royal Ballet, where he danced until 2001, forming a strong relationship with choreographer Kenneth MacMillan, who created roles for him in *Winter Dreams* and *The Judas Tree*. Since retiring from the stage, he now directs and choreographs internationally.

Irek Mukhamedov in the title role of the ballet Spartacus.

- CHAPTER FIVE -

FAMOUS BALLETS

*When you go and see a ballet, it sometimes helps to know
the story beforehand so you can follow what's going on.
Here are the stories of some famous ballets.*

*Opposite: Iohna Loots as Clara and Ricardo Cervera as
Hans-Peter travel to the magical Land of Sweets in
Act I of The Nutcracker.*

GISELLE

- A ROMANTIC BALLET -

This is one of the earliest ballets still performed as part of the repertory of major ballet companies. It is regarded as the classic Romantic ballet!

The story

ACT I shows Giselle, a peasant girl, falling in love with a stranger who comes to her village. He is Count Albrecht but he doesn't tell her his real name. A local lad, Hilarion, is in love with Giselle. He discovers who Albrecht really is but Giselle does not believe him. Then some nobles pass by, including Albrecht's fiancée Bathilde. Bathilde tells Giselle that she is engaged to Albrecht, revealing his true identity, and Giselle is shocked. She stabs herself with Albrecht's sword and dies.

The corps de ballet dance as the Wilis, the vengeful ghosts of abandoned girls who dance men to death.

ACT II takes place at night. Hilarion visits Giselle's grave where the Wilis, ghosts of girls who were abandoned and died before their wedding day, rise to haunt him, led by Myrtha, their queen. They are full of revenge and dance to death any man they find. The Wilis chase Hilarion to his death and then fall upon Albrecht. Giselle tries to save him as he becomes exhausted. At last, dawn breaks and the Wilis' power is destroyed. Giselle's spirit is free as her mercy to Albrecht has stopped her from becoming a Wili herself. She returns to her grave, leaving Albrecht alive but alone and in sorrow.

Carlotta Grisi, who created the title role of Giselle.

Roberta Marquez dances the role of Giselle.

BALLET FACTS

Date: 1841; Paris Opéra, France

Music: Adolphe Adam, also known for the ballet *Le Corsaire*

Choreography: Marius Petipa, based on earlier work by Jean Coralli and Jules Perrot

About the ballet: Italian ballerina Carlotta Grisi was the first to dance the role of Giselle. The ballet caused a sensation and made Grisi a huge star. It also became Adolphe Adam's most famous work, especially notable for his mysterious music of the Wilis in Act II.

- THE -
SLEEPING BEAUTY
- A CLASSICAL BALLET -

BALLET FACTS

Date: 1890; Mariinsky Theater, St. Petersburg, Russia

Music: Pyotr Il'yich Tchaikovsky

Choreography: Marius Petipa

About the ballet: This was the second ballet that Tchaikovsky composed the music for, his first being *Swan Lake*. The ballet contains the famous Rose Adage in Act I, one of the most difficult sequences in ballet, when Aurora is presented to her four suitors and has to balance unsupported on one leg and on pointe throughout.

Oⁿᴱ ᴏꜰ ᴛʜᴇ ɢʀᴇᴀᴛ Rᴜꜱꜱɪᴀɴ ᴄʟᴀꜱꜱɪᴄꜱ, ᴛʜɪꜱ ᴡᴇʟʟ-ʟᴏᴠᴇᴅ ꜰᴀɪʀʏ-ᴛᴀʟᴇ ballet has been delighting audiences for over 100 years. It is also one of The Royal Ballet's best-known works.

The story

The Prologue opens at Princess Aurora's christening. The king and queen have invited fairies to be godmothers. But they forgot to invite Carabosse—she is angry and declares that one day Aurora will prick her finger and die. Luckily, the Lilac Fairy still has a gift to give. She vows that Aurora will not die but sleep for a hundred years, to be awakened only by a prince's kiss.

ACT I takes place when Aurora has grown up. It's her birthday and four suitors have come to propose to her. But during the party, Aurora finds an old woman who gives her a spindle from a spinning wheel. She dances with it and suddenly pricks her finger! Carabosse appears triumphant but the Lilac Fairy then sends the court to sleep. An enchanted forest grows around the palace.

ACT II happens one hundred years later. A Prince is hunting in the forest. The Lilac Fairy shows him a vision of Aurora sleeping. The vision dances with him and when it disappears, he begs the Lilac Fairy to take him to this sleeping beauty. She leads him to the palace, where they find Aurora. He kisses her and she wakes, along with the rest of the court.

ACT III is a wedding party. Aurora and the Prince get married, with all the courtiers in attendance. Everyone dances at the celebration and the Lilac Fairy gives her blessing to the royal couple.

Emma Maguire as The Fairy of the Golden Vine, one of the good fairies who become Princess Aurora's godmothers. An important part of her dance is the quick finger pointing, which shows her joy at the birth of the baby.

Hikaru Kobayashi as Princess Aurora performing part of the Rose Adage. Her four suitors hold her in turn, but she has to balance unsupported between each hold.

Lauren Cuthbertson as Princess Aurora, and her four suitors, after she has completed the Rose Adage.

SWAN LAKE
- A CLASSICAL BALLET -

THIS IS ONE OF THE BEST-LOVED BALLETS OF ALL TIME. Its costumes, choreography, and music are unforgettable, and it continues to be included in the repertory of ballet companies worldwide.

The corps de ballet dancing the Swans in Act II of **Swan Lake.**

The story

ACT I tells the story of Prince Siegfried. He is expected to marry but he doesn't want to marry a girl he doesn't love. On his birthday, his friends give him a crossbow as a gift. He sees some swans fly past and Siegfried's friend Benno suggests shooting them with the crossbow. They leave in pursuit!

ACT II is set by the lake in moonlight. Benno looks for the swans while Siegfried is left alone. Suddenly Von Rothbart, an evil spirit, appears disguised as an owl. One of the swans arrives and turns into a beautiful girl—Odette. Odette tells Siegfried that she and her companions are under Von Rothbart's spell and can only be human at night. The spell can be broken if someone swears undying love for her. Siegfried gives her his promise but dawn comes and she turns back into a swan.

ACT III takes place at the prince's castle. He must choose a bride from six princesses but he keeps thinking of Odette and cannot choose. Von Rothbart appears with his daughter Odile, whom he has disguised to look like Odette. Odile and Siegfried dance and he believes her to be Odette. Under Von Rothbart's spell, he swears his love for her and at that moment, the real Odette appears in a mirror. Siegfried has broken his vow and it is now too late to save her!

ACT IV is set again by the lake. Odette wants to drown herself but Siegfried arrives and begs for her forgiveness. She forgives him but nothing can change the fact that he has broken his vow and she must remain a swan. They decide to die together and Odette throws herself into the lake. Von Rothbart tries to stop Siegfried from following but fails. Dawn breaks and the couple are united in death and love.

Zenaida Yanowsky and Nehemiah Kish in the principal roles of Odile and Prince Siegfried in **Swan Lake.**

Music and choreography

Little is known about the exact origins of *Swan Lake* as few original records survive. However, we do know that Pyotr Il'yich Tchaikovsky was commissioned to compose the music for the ballet in 1875 by Vladimir Begichev, who was a supervisor of the Russian Imperial Theaters in Moscow. Tchaikovsky himself had a lot of control over the story and he is thought to have been inspired by Russian folklore and ancient legends of swan maidens.

The original production of the ballet wasn't a great success as the choreography wasn't rated very highly. After Tchaikovsky's death, the ballet was revived and given new choreography by Marius Petipa and Lev Ivanov. It is this version that most modern productions are based on. It has enchanting scenes with highly memorable pieces, including the cygnets' dance in Act II and The Black Swan pas de deux in Act III

*Fonteyn and Nureyev
in rehearsal.*

BALLET FACTS

Swan Lake is one of the most performed ballets of all time and the roles of Odette/Odile and Prince Siegfried have been performed by many of ballet's great partnerships.
Highlights include:

*Margot Fonteyn
and Rudolf Nureyev*

Royal Ballet superstars, Fonteyn and Nureyev had a dance partnership that lasted 26 years, from 1962 to 1988.

*Antoinette Sibley
and Anthony Dowell*

Sibley and Dowell were one of the great partnerships of the 1960s and 1970s and created many famous roles.

*Sylvie Guillem
and Jonathan Cope*

Guillem and Cope danced many leading roles together from the late 1980s until 2006, when Cope retired. Cope was the perfect partner for Guillem, as they were both tall dancers.

*Artists of the corps de ballet in their dressing room before Act II of The Royal Ballet's **Swan Lake** in 1987.*

- THE -
NUTCRACKER
- A CLASSICAL BALLET -

*Dancers of The Royal Ballet in the Chinese dance from Act II of **The Nutcracker**. It is performed by Clara and four male dancers, who dance around her in a comical way.*

THIS WONDERFUL CLASSICAL BALLET IS TRADITIONALLY performed at Christmas, as it is set during a Christmas party—and has a wonderful scene of dancing snowflakes at the end of Act I!

The story

ACT I opens with a Christmas party at the home of children Clara and Fritz. A magician, called Herr Drosselmeyer, has been invited to entertain the children and their friends. He brings presents, including a Nutcracker Doll for Clara, inside which his nephew, Hans-Peter, is imprisoned by the Mouse Queen's spell. After the party, Clara wakes in the night and looks for her doll. Strange things now happen—the whole room grows, including the Christmas tree. Mice appear, led by a Mouse King. The Nutcracker comes to life and leads an army of toy soldiers to fight the mice. Clara helps to defeat the Mouse King and the Nutcracker Doll turns back into his real self, Hans-Peter, dancing with her and taking her to a magical land on a sleigh, where snowflakes dance through the night sky.

ACT II shows Clara and Hans-Peter transported into the Land of Sweets, conjured by Drosselmeyer. The Sugar Plum Fairy and her Prince arrive and Drosselmeyer shows Clara dances from around the world: Spain, Arabia, China, Russia, and the Mirlitons dance from France. The entertainment finishes with the dance of the flowers and the Sugar Plum Fairy dances with her Prince before Clara and Hans-Peter return home.

*The Arabian dance from Act II of **The Nutcracker**. The music is slow and exotic as the ballerina is presented by three male dancers in turn, showing a variety of holds and carrying her high above their heads.*

*Sarah Lamb as the Sugar Plum Fairy. The role of the Sugar Plum Fairy incorporates a highly technical solo and pas de deux to some of the best-known music in **The Nutcracker**.*

BALLET FACTS

Date: 1892; Mariinsky Theater, St. Petersburg, Russia

Music: Pyotr Il'yich Tchaikovsky

Choreography: Marius Petipa and Lev Ivanov

About the ballet: The ballet was taken from a story originally by E.T.A. Hoffmann. Act II is filled with contrast provided by short dances from around the world. These dances are known as **divertissements**—pieces of music for a small group of dancers that aren't always connected to the main storyline. Many versions of the ballet have been choreographed over the years—often with different interpretations of the original.

THE
FIREBIRD
- A NEOCLASSICAL BALLET -

THIS WAS THE FIRST BALLET COMPOSED BY IGOR STRAVINSKY, commissioned for the Ballets Russes. A ballet in one act, it was an instant success. Neoclassical ballet means that its style belongs to Classical ballet of the early 20th century.

The story

The Firebird tells the story of Prince Ivan, who enters the magical garden of The Immortal Kostcheï, who casts spells on passing travelers. In the garden, Ivan chases the Firebird and catches her. In return for her freedom, she gives one of her feathers to him and agrees to help him if he is in trouble.

Finding himself at the gate of an old castle, Ivan meets some princesses and falls in love with one of them. Kostcheï and his weird creatures try to capture Ivan. The Firebird keeps her promise and bewitches the creatures, making them perform an energetic dance, known as the Infernal Dance, and then sends them to sleep.

Eventually, the Firebird tells Ivan the secret of Kostcheï's immortality—his soul is contained inside a huge, magical egg. Ivan destroys the egg which kills Kostcheï. All the magical creatures turn into real beings and awake, including the Princesses. The ballet ends with Ivan and his chosen Princess getting married, while everyone joins in the celebrations.

Roberta Marquez and Valeri Hristov as the Firebird and Prince Ivan in The Royal Ballet's production of Stravinsky's first ballet. Look at the position of the ballerina's fluttering hands.

BALLET FACTS

Date: 1910; Paris Opéra, France

Music: Igor Stravinsky

Choreography: Mikhail Fokine

About the ballet: The ballet is based on the Russian folktale about the Firebird, a powerful spirit whose feathers give beauty and protection to the Earth. Well known for the fluttering dance of the Firebird itself and the wedding celebration at the end, the ballet gave Stravinsky international fame.

*Bennet Gartside and Artists of The Royal Ballet in the 2012 performance of **The Firebird**.*

- THE NUTCRACKER -

Along with *Swan Lake*, *The Nutcracker* is perhaps the world's most beloved ballet. Here, Iohna Loots as Clara joins Artists of The Royal Ballet in the Dance of the Mirlitons, also known as the Dance of the Reed Pipes, in Act II.

CINDERELLA

- A CLASSICAL BALLET -

THIS BALLET ORIGINALLY PREMIERED IN 1893 AND HAS since inspired many different choreographers to produce their own versions, including Frederick Ashton, whose production to music by Prokofiev was the first full-length British ballet.

The story

ACT I Cinderella lives with her father and two nasty stepsisters. The sisters are getting ready to go to a ball but Cinderella is not invited. An old woman comes to the door begging and Cinderella takes pity on her and gives her some bread. The sisters leave for the ball, leaving Cinderella alone and sad. The old woman reappears and turns into Cinderella's fairy godmother. Cinderella's rags turn into a beautiful dress and a pumpkin becomes her coach.

ACT II takes place in the ballroom at the Prince's palace. The court jester is waiting for the ball to begin and makes fun of the stepsisters. Cinderella's carriage approaches and she makes a grand entrance. The Prince is enchanted with her but at the stroke of midnight her dress turns to rags and she runs away, leaving behind her slipper.

ACT III shows Cinderella back in the kitchen. She thinks the ball was all a dream but when she finds a sparkling slipper in her apron, she realizes it was true. The Prince arrives with the lost slipper, in search of its owner. The stepsisters try it on but with no luck. Suddenly, Cinderella's other slipper falls out of her apron and the Prince knows she is the girl he is looking for!

Luke Heydon, Gary Avis, and Wayne Sleep in The Royal Ballet's 2010 performance of Ashton's **Cinderella.**

Ashton (left) and Helpmann (right) as the stepsisters in **Cinderella,** *1949. Cinderella is played by Margot Fonteyn.*

BALLET FACTS

Date: 1948, Royal Opera House, UK   *Music:* Sergey Prokofiev
Choreography: Frederick Ashton

About the ballet: This was Ashton's first full-length ballet. He decided to create his version in a very British way, with lots of pantomime and comedy tradition. He originally danced one of the step-sisters himself, with the other danced by Robert Helpmann, who later played the role of the Child Catcher in the famous film *Chitty Chitty Bang Bang.*

ROMEO AND JULIET
- A CLASSICAL BALLET -

BASED ON ONE ON OF SHAKESPEARE'S MOST memorable plays, *Romeo and Juliet* tells the tale of two young lovers.

The story

ACT I opens in the Italian city of Verona. Romeo is a Montague and Juliet is a Capulet and the two families are sworn enemies. However, there is a ball happening at the Capulets' house and Romeo and his friends decide to go. He meets Juliet. Later, Juliet appears on her balcony and sees Romeo in the garden below. They declare their love for one another.

ACT II shows the lovers getting married secretly. Romeo and Juliet are married by Friar Laurence. But later Juliet's cousin Tybalt fights with Romeo's friend Mercutio and kills him. In turn, Romeo kills Tybalt and is banished from Verona.

ACT III opens with the lovers parting at dawn. Juliet's parents want her to marry Paris, but Juliet loves Romeo. She seeks the help of Friar Laurence who gives her a sleeping potion which will make her parents believe she has died. He then sends a message to Romeo to come to the family tomb, where Juliet's body has been "buried," so that Romeo can escape with her. But Romeo doesn't get the message, and on hearing that Juliet has died, comes to find her body and poisons himself. Juliet wakes up and on finding Romeo is dead, she stabs herself.

Federico Bonelli as Romeo, with his friends Mercutio (Alexander Campbell) and Benvolio (Dawid Trzensimiech).

Evgenia Obraztsova and Steven McRae in Romeo and Juliet, 2012.

BALLET FACTS

Date: 1965, Royal Opera House, UK

Music: Sergey Prokofiev

Choreography: Kenneth MacMillan

About the ballet: Prokofiev's music has been made into a ballet by several choreographers, and this version for The Royal Ballet was Kenneth MacMillan's first three-act ballet. The premiere, with Margot Fonteyn and Rudolf Nureyev, received 43 curtain calls!

ALICE'S
- ADVENTURES IN -
WONDERLAND
- A CLASSICAL BALLET -

Beatriz Stix-Brunell as Alice and the corps de ballet as the Wonderland creatures in The Royal Ballet's 2013 performances of Alice's Adventures in Wonderland. Masks and wigs show the animal characteristics of the creatures.

BASED ON LEWIS CARROLL'S BOOK *ALICE'S ADVENTURES IN WONDERLAND*, this was Christopher Wheeldon's first full-length work for The Royal Ballet and the Company's first full-length ballet commissioned for 16 years.

The story

ACT I opens in Oxford on a summer afternoon. The Liddell family are about to host a garden party. Alice's mother accuses Jack the gardener of stealing jam tarts and sends him away. Alice, who is fond of Jack, is devastated but a friend of the family, Lewis Carroll, consoles her by offering to take her photograph. He disappears beneath the camera cloth and emerges as a White Rabbit! When he bounds into his camera-bag and vanishes, Alice follows him and lands with a thump in a mysterious corridor. Through a keyhole Alice spies a magical garden, though the door is locked and she can't get to it. Jack transforms into the Knave of Hearts and he and the White Rabbit lead Alice into many strange adventures.

ACT II shows more of Alice's adventures. Alice finds herself at the bizarre tea party of the Mad Hatter. She then escapes and finds herself in the garden she was searching for. The Knave appears but the Queen of Hearts and her guards are chasing him, as he is accused of stealing jam tarts. Furious, the Queen orders the capture of the Knave, but he escapes. The White Rabbit dashes after them, taking Alice with him.

ACT III takes place in the garden of the Queen of Hearts. The Queen orders the gardeners to be executed for accidentally planting white roses. While the Executioner is distracted, Alice and the White Rabbit smuggle the gardeners out of sight. The Knave rejoins Alice, but he is found and the Queen orders him to the castle to face trial. The witnesses are brought in and Alice insists the Knave is innocent. Together, they deliver a final testimony and win the hearts of everyone but the Queen, who seizes an ax in order to kill the Knave. With no escape in view, Alice pushes a witness over. He falls on top of another, who then falls on another, and the whole court collapses... they're only playing cards, after all!

BALLET FACTS

Date: 2011

Music: Joby Talbot

Choreography: Christopher Wheeldon

About the ballet: The wildly imaginative world of Wonderland is brought to life in this ballet with its colorful sets, puppets, projections, masks, and inventive choreography. Among its highlights are a tap-dancing Mad Hatter, and a comic version of the Rose Adage based on *The Sleeping Beauty*, danced by the crazy Queen of Hearts.

Tamara Rojo as the Queen of Hearts in the 2011 performances.

RAVEN GIRL

- A MODERN BALLET -

Sarah Lamb as Raven Girl, after her character has been fitted with the wings she longs for.

A BALLET IN ONE ACT, *RAVEN GIRL* IS A MODERN FAIRYTALE. Although it is a contemporary work, in some ways it follows the traditions of the great story ballets. Like *Swan Lake*, it tells of a girl who is half bird and half human.

The story

A Postman finds a fledgling Raven, who has fallen out of a nest. He worries that she's hurt, so he takes her home and cares for her. Gradually the Postman and the Raven fall in love and, eventually, they have a child—a human girl with the soul of a bird. Her parents love her completely but she longs to be with others like her. But she's the only Raven Girl in the world and there is no one else like her! She feels imprisoned by her arms and legs. She has difficulty making friends at school because she doesn't fit in—she speaks with a harsh voice and she plays different games than the other children.

When she grows older, the Raven Girl goes to university and learns about chimeras (creatures with body parts from different animals) from a visiting doctor. She decides to ask him whether he can perform an operation to give her wings and he agrees to do it. The operation is a success but being a girl with wings isn't easy. However, the Raven Girl overcomes her difficulties and finds a Raven Prince she can find true happiness with.

BALLET FACTS

Date: 2013

Music: Gabriel Yared

Choreography: Wayne McGregor

About the ballet: This ballet is a collaboration with author and visual artist Audrey Niffenegger and choreographer Wayne McGregor. The author came up with the characters, story, and images, with input from the choreographer, to inspire the music, design, and choreography. Part of the set also uses video projections, a technique often used in modern ballets.

*Sarah Lamb as Raven Girl and Eric Underwood as the Prince in Wayne McGregor's **Raven Girl**, 2013.*

WATCHING BALLET

Once you discover the spectacular world of ballet, you can't help wanting more! Whether you are a dancer or whether you just enjoy being in the audience, watching ballet is an exciting thing to do.

Go live!

Large cities have big theaters where you can watch top ballet companies perform live. However, tickets can sometimes be expensive and it might be difficult for you to get there. A good alternative is to go and watch a touring company at a smaller theater nearby. Many companies tour regularly so look out for advertising posters or go online and see what your local theaters have coming up.

*Frederick Ashton's **La Fille mal gardée** is good to go and see if you are new to ballet. It is full of good humor and energetic choreography and is inspired by nature. Here, in the 2010 performance, Roberta Marquez dances the role of Lise and Steven McRae is Colas.*

*Elizabeth Harrod in a scene from the 2009 performance of **The Nutcracker**—one of the world's favorite ballets and a glittering performance that is wonderful to watch at Christmas time!*

A treat at the movies!

Another way to see ballet is at a movie theater! While a ballet is taking place live on stage at a big theater, cameras relay the show to cinemas in other cities and even other countries, so that many people can join in the experience at the same time. You can watch The Royal Ballet from your hometown—and you might even be able to watch the Bolshoi Ballet live from Moscow!

Watching on TV

Occasionally, ballet productions are featured on TV but the easiest way to watch is on DVD. Most famous ballets are available on DVD so you should be able to choose your favorites. If you've never seen a ballet before, good ones to try are *The Nutcracker*, *Coppélia*, or *The Tales of Beatrix Potter*.

*Miyako Yoshida and Carlos Acosta in The Royal Ballet's performance of **Coppélia** that was broadcast live by the BBC in 2000.*

Darcey Bussell as Sylvia in The Royal Ballet's production of the same name.

DARCEY BUSSELL

BORN: 1969   **NATIONALITY:** British

At age 13, Darcey Bussell joined The Royal Ballet School. In 1987, at age 18, she joined Sadler's Wells Royal Ballet and then moved to The Royal Ballet one year later. At just 20 years old, she became a Principal dancer when Kenneth MacMillan created the leading role for her in his version of *The Prince of the Pagodas* in 1989. She then remained with The Royal Ballet for her entire career during which she danced many leading roles, such as Cinderella and Princess Aurora in *The Sleeping Beauty*. She also danced as a guest artist with world-leading companies, including New York City Ballet and The Australian Ballet.

JONATHAN COPE

BORN: 1963   **NATIONALITY:** British

Jonathan Cope trained in Wales before attending The Royal Ballet School. He joined The Royal Ballet in 1982 and was promoted to Principal in 1986. His repertory included Prince Siegfried in *Swan Lake*, Albrecht in *Giselle*, the Prince in *Cinderella* and in *The Nutcracker*, plus many other roles including the Salamander Prince dancing opposite Darcey Bussell in MacMillan's premiere of *The Prince of the Pagodas*. He retired from dancing in 2006 and is now a repetiteur for The Royal Ballet.

*Jonathan Cope as The Prince in **Cinderella**.*

- THE DREAM -

Roberta Marquez as Titania and Steven McRae as Oberon, king and queen of the fairies, in Frederick Ashton's *The Dream*. The ballet is based on Shakespeare's well-loved play *A Midsummer Night's Dream* and was created to celebrate the 400th anniversary of his birth in 1964.

GLOSSARY

ABSTRACT BALLET
A ballet with no specific story or theme, which is united only by the dancers' movements.

AUDITION
A short performance that a dancer does as a test in front of an examiner or director, in order to win a place in a school, company, or specific role in a ballet.

AUDITORIUM
The space in the theater where the audience sits to watch the performance.

BALLETS DE COUR
Court dances that are now considered to be the first ballets, performed in the courts of France and Italy during the 15th to 17th centuries.

BARRE
A wooden handrail, normally fixed to the wall in a rehearsal studio, that dancers hold when they are practicing certain steps and positions.

CHOREOGRAPHER
The person who invents sequences of steps for a dance. He or she usually also decides how the dance is presented, in terms of music, costume, and sets.

CLASS
The daily training session that dancers take part in.

CLASSICAL BALLET
A formal style of ballet, which originated in France and then developed during the 19th century in Russia. Classical ballet is based on set positions of the arms, feet, and body.

CONTEMPORARY DANCE
A style of dance that developed in the 20th century that combines elements of different dance styles. It emphasizes improvisation and a wide range of movements, rather than the formal structure of Classical ballet.

CORPS DE BALLET
The dancers in a ballet company who perform large group dances.

DEMI PLIÉ
A bend of the knees, which a dancer performs in ballet, with legs turned out and heels on the ground.

DIVERTISSEMENTS
Pieces of music for small groups of dancers to perform to, which are not necessarily connected to the main story in a ballet but used simply as set pieces for the audience to enjoy.

JETÉ
A big jump from one foot to another, performed in ballet.

MIME
Acting or expressing ideas and emotions by using gestures, rather than words or sound.

NEOCLASSICAL BALLET
A style of dance from the early 20th century, shown in the works of the Ballets Russes and George Balanchine. It uses the formal moves of Classical ballet but without the drama and elaborate detail of the 19th century story ballets.

ON POINTE
A ballerina's technique of balancing on the very tips of her toes. Very occasionally used by male dancers, too.

PAS DE DEUX
A dance sequence performed by a male and female couple.

POINTE SHOES
Ballet shoes that are specially designed with stiff toes in order to enable a ballerina to dance on pointe.

PREMIERE
The first time ever that a ballet is performed.

PRINCIPAL DANCERS
The most senior dancers in a ballet company, who perform solos and dance the lead roles.

REPERTORY
A collection of ballets frequently performed by a company or dancer.

ROMANTIC BALLET
A ballet created in the early 19th century or in that style, which follows the tradition of the artistic movement known as Romanticism. Among other things, Romanticism placed value on strength of emotion and the beauty of wild nature.

STORY BALLET
A ballet that tells a story, such as *Cinderella*.

THEME BALLET
A ballet that is united by a theme—an idea or subject that holds the ballet together.

WINGS
The areas to the side of the stage where the dancers warm up and wait to go on stage during a performance.